TEAM SPIRIT®

SMART BOOKS FOR YOUNG FANS

THE BUFFALO BILLS

BY
MARK STEWART

NORWOODHOUSE PRESS

CHICAGO, ILLINOIS

Norwood House Press
P.O. Box 316598
Chicago, Illinois 60631

For information regarding Norwood House Press, please visit our website at:
www.norwoodhousepress.com or call 866-565-2900.

All photos courtesy of Getty Images except the following:
SportsChrome (4, 14, 32), Topps, Inc. (6, 10, 15, 16, 17, 34 both, 36, 37, 38, 42 top, 43 top),
Cord Communications Corp. (7), Beckett Publications (23, 42 bottom), Editions Rencontre (25),
Black Book Partners (28, 40, 45), Author's Collection (33), Lexington Library, Inc. (35 top left),
Buffalo Bills/NFL (35 bottom, 43 bottom), McDonald's Corp. (39),
The Sporting News (41), Matt Richman (48).
Cover Photo: SportsChrome

The memorabilia and artifacts pictured in this book are presented for educational and informational purposes,
and come from the collection of the author.

Editor: Mike Kennedy
Designer: Ron Jaffe
Project Management: Black Book Partners, LLC.
Special thanks to Topps, Inc.

Library of Congress Cataloging-in-Publication Data

Stewart, Mark, 1960-
   The Buffalo Bills / by Mark Stewart.
      p. cm. -- (Team spirit)
   Includes bibliographical references and index.
   Summary: "A Team Spirit Football edition featuring the Buffalo Bills that
chronicles the history and accomplishments of the team. Includes access to
the Team Spirit website which provides additional information and
photos"--Provided by publisher.
   ISBN 978-1-59953-515-9 (library edition : alk. paper) -- ISBN
978-1-60357-457-0 (ebook)
   1. Buffalo Bills (Football team)--History--Juvenile literature. I. Title.

GV956.B83S84 2012
796.332'640974797--dc23
                                              2012012041

Manufactured in the United States of America in North Mankato, Minnesota.
205N—082012

COVER PHOTO: The Bills celebrate a win during the 2011 season.

Table of Contents

ABOUT OUR GLOSSARY

In this book, there may be several words that you are reading for the first time. Some are sports words, some are new vocabulary words, and some are familiar words that are used in an unusual way. All of these words are defined on page 46. Throughout the book, sports words appear in **bold type**. Regular vocabulary words appear in ***bold italic type***.

Meet the Bills

Can a football team take on the personality of the city where it plays? Fans of the Buffalo Bills know the answer to that question. In every victory by the team, there is satisfaction in knowing that hard work has its rewards. In every defeat, there is a valuable lesson to be learned. This is true whether you are a Buffalo player … or a Buffalo fan.

That is why the Bills are at their most exciting—and most dangerous—when things look their worst. No team is better at fighting back when they are behind. In fact, the Bills seem to specialize in amazing comebacks.

This book tells the story of the Bills. They win by playing 60 minutes of tough football. Everyone on the team is ready to contribute when a game starts, and no one holds back when the Bills take the field. That is what it means to play football in Buffalo.

The Bills greet running back Fred Jackson before kickoff time. Every Buffalo player is ready to contribute once the game starts.

Glory Days

Back in the 1950s, *professional* football was on the rise. The **National Football League (NFL)** was adding millions of new fans every year. The sport was so popular that a rival league called the **American Football League (AFL)** began play. In 1959, businessman Ralph Wilson bought a team in the AFL. After considering his options, Wilson turned to a town that he knew really wanted his team, Buffalo, New York. The Bills were born. Buffalo was no stranger to pro football. The Bills were the city's fourth team. The first club played in the NFL during the 1920s.

In the 1960s, coach Lou Saban and a smart quarterback named Jack Kemp led the Bills. Kemp's favorite receiver was Elbert Dubenion, who specialized in catching long passes. Buffalo had a strong running game powered by running back Cookie Gilchrist and linemen Billy Shaw and Stew Barber. Tom Sestak and George Saimes led the defense.

The Bills quickly rose to the top of the AFL. In 1964, they won the league championship in a tight game with the San Diego Chargers. The following year, Buffalo faced San Diego again for the AFL title. The Bills repeated as champions.

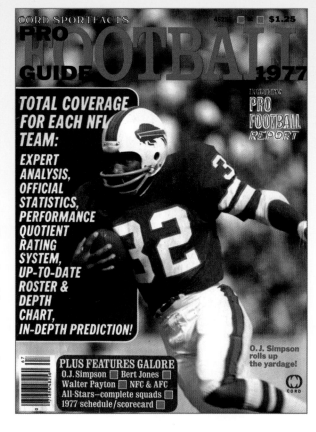

In 1970, the Bills were one of 10 AFL teams to join the NFL. By then, they had football's most exciting player, O.J. Simpson. He was a swift and explosive running back who had the league's best blockers in front of him. Simpson was nicknamed the "Juice," and his offensive line was known as the "Electric Company." In 1973, Simpson became the first player in history to rush for more than 2,000 yards in a season.

Despite all its talent, Buffalo won just once in the **playoffs** from 1966 to 1987. The team had three great "Joes" during

LEFT: This trading card shows the 1960 Bills.   **ABOVE**: O.J. Simpson was on dozens of magazine covers during his years with the Bills.

this period—Joe Ferguson, Joe DeLamielleure, and Joe Cribbs. However, the Bills were no match for strong clubs such as the Miami Dolphins, Pittsburgh Steelers, and Oakland Raiders.

Buffalo's luck began to change when coach Marv Levy and quarterback Jim Kelly joined the team in 1986. Levy was thoughtful and friendly. But when he stepped on the field, he was all business. His teams matched his personality, and Buffalo soon became a powerhouse.

The Bills had an extremely talented defense. Its leaders included Bruce Smith, Darryl Talley, Shane Conlan, and Cornelius Bennett. Smith gave Buffalo a big advantage with his passion for football and his ability to **sack** the quarterback. On offense, Kelly was the perfect leader for the Bills. Few passers in the NFL could match his strong and accurate throwing arm. He got plenty of help from running back Thurman Thomas and Andre Reed. When Buffalo needed an extra spark, receiver Steve Tasker usually provided it.

LEFT: Bruce Smith celebrates a sack.
ABOVE: Jim Kelly gets words of advice from coach Marv Levy.

The Bills were the best team in the **American Football Conference (AFC)** in the 1990s. During one stretch, they played in the **Super Bowl** four years in a row. Unfortunately, Buffalo lost each time it went to the big game.

As so often happens in sports, after many winning seasons, the Bills began to struggle. Kelly retired in 1997, and Levy left the following year. After making the playoffs in 1998 and 1999, the Bills went more than 10 seasons without returning to the **postseason**. The team hired several coaches, but none of them came close to matching Levy's success.

Still, the Bills put plenty of talent on the field. Bryce Paup, Sam Cowart, Takeo Spikes, Terence McGee, and Aaron Schobel were among the top defenders in the NFL. Eric Moulds, Lee Evans, Travis Henry, and Peerless Price were exciting players on offense. Despite great performances from these stars, the Bills lost more games than they won.

As Buffalo fans came to realize, a winning team needs to build around a confident and skilled quarterback. Kelly had been one of the game's top passers. Finding another leader like him was no easy

task. In 2009, Ryan Fitzpatrick joined the Bills. Fitzpatrick was known as one of the most intelligent players in football. In Buffalo, he showed that his arm was just as strong as his mind.

Working with receiver Stevie Johnson and running back Fred Jackson, Fitzpatrick brought a new attitude to the Buffalo offense. Nick Barnett and Mario Williams did the same for the defense. The Bills began to beat some of the best teams in the NFL. It gave them the shot of confidence that every young team needs. As the Bills and their fans look forward, they know it's only a matter of time before they return to the winning ways of the past.

LEFT: This trading card shows Bryce Paup in action.
ABOVE: Ryan Fitzpatrick spots an open receiver.

Home Turf

From 1960 to 1972, the Bills played in War Memorial Stadium, which had been built during the 1930s. In 1973, the Bills moved into a new home. For many years, it was called Rich Stadium, after a local food company that helped *finance* the project. In 1998, it was renamed Ralph Wilson Stadium, after the Bills' owner. It has been enlarged and *modernized* several times since then.

Although it can be very chilly on winter days in Buffalo, Bills fans love to watch football in their stadium. It features three tiers of blue and red seats, including sections with heated chairs and enclosed areas designed for comfortable viewing. The playing field is 50 feet below ground level, so fans in the upper deck do not have to climb too high to get to their seats.

BY THE NUMBERS

- The Bills' stadium has 73,079 seats.
- The upper deck seats are 110 feet above the playing field.
- In 2007, the team unveiled a video scoreboard that is 33.5 feet high and 82.8 feet wide.

The sun is out for a game at Ralph Wilson Stadium.

Dressed for Success

Blue has been Buffalo's main color since the team's first season in 1960. Back then, the Bills wore a light blue jersey with silver helmets. The following year, they introduced a new uniform that is similar to today's version. It featured a dark blue jersey with red and white stripes on the shoulders. The helmet was white with a red buffalo on each side.

The team used this helmet design until 1974, when a modern-looking blue buffalo with a red streak took its place. During the 1980s, the Bills changed to red helmets. In 2002, they switched their uniform color to an even darker shade of blue.

The Bills took their name from Buffalo's team in the old **All-America Football Conference (AAFC)** of the 1940s. Owner Ralph Wilson loved the name—even though it has nothing to do with the city. "Bills" refers to "Buffalo Bill" Cody, an entertainer who traveled the country in the 1800s with his Wild West show.

JACK KEMP
QUARTERBACK

LEFT: Stevie Johnson warms up in the team's 2011 uniform.
RIGHT: Jack Kemp models the Bills' jersey from the 1960s.

We Won!

MIKE STRATTON
BUFFALO BILLS   LINEBACKER

There is an old saying in football that defense wins championships. In the early days of the American Football League, the Bills proved that this was true. While other AFL teams tried to put lots of points on the scoreboard, Buffalo focused on keeping opponents out of the end zone. During the early 1960s, the Bills had the AFL's best defense. When they had the ball, they controlled the game with a steady ground attack. That **strategy** led to a pair of AFL titles.

In 1964, the Bills finished 12–2 and earned a place in the **AFL Championship Game**. Playing before a noisy home crowd, they faced the San Diego Chargers and their star running back, Keith Lincoln. The first time the Chargers had the ball, Lincoln sliced through the Buffalo defense for a 38-yard gain. Moments later, San Diego scored to take a 7–0 lead. It was a different story the next

WRAY CARLTON halfback

time the Chargers had the ball. Lincoln caught a short pass, but linebacker Mike Stratton was waiting for him. Stratton made a hard tackle, forcing Lincoln to leave the game. San Diego's offense struggled the rest of the day.

The Bills took a 13–7 lead in the first half on two **field goals** by Pete Gogolak and a touchdown run by Wray Carlton. In the final period, Jack Kemp threw a 48-yard pass to Glenn Bass, who was tackled one yard short of the goal line. Kemp then scored the game's final touchdown on a **quarterback sneak**. The Bills won 20–7 to become AFL champions.

One year later, the Bills met the Chargers again for the title, this time in San Diego. Buffalo surprised the Chargers by lining up on offense with two tight ends. The Bills also confused San Diego with some creative defensive strategies.

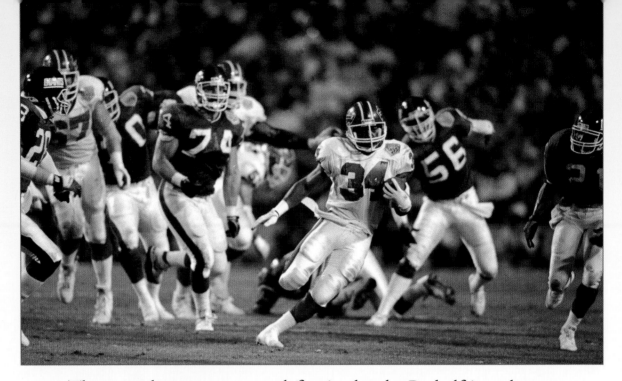

The game began as a tense defensive battle. By halftime, however, the Bills had taken a 14–0 lead. The key play was a 74-yard punt return by Butch Byrd for a touchdown. In the second half, Buffalo increased the pressure on defense, while Kemp guided the team on three time-consuming drives. Each one ended with a field goal by Gogolak. The final score was 23–0. The Bills celebrated their second title in a row.

The Bills played for the AFL championship again in 1966, but they were beaten by the Kansas City Chiefs. A merger between the AFL and the NFL had just been announced, and the winner of the game was to play in the first Super Bowl. The Bills missed this chance at history and had to wait until the 1990 season before they finally reached their first Super Bowl.

Starting that season, the team rewarded the patience of its fans by winning the AFC championship four years in a row. The Bills put together the most dangerous offense in the NFL. Jim Kelly was one of the league's best passers. Thurman Thomas was a great runner who was also a good receiver. Andre Reed and James Lofton combined to give Buffalo a deadly pass-catching duo down the field.

The defense could be just as scary. Shane Conlan made tackles all over the field. Bruce Smith, Cornelius Bennett, and Darryl Talley put constant pressure on opposing quarterbacks. Nate Odomes led the **secondary**.

Unfortunately, the Bills lost in the Super Bowl each time—to the New York Giants, Washington Redskins, and Dallas Cowboys twice. They led in three of these games but fell short in their quest for a championship. The loss to the Giants was the most painful. Thomas was unstoppable, running for 135 yards and catching five passes for another 55 yards. Buffalo had a chance to win on the last play of the game, but Scott Norwood's field goal attempt sailed wide right.

LEFT: Thurman Thomas runs for daylight against the New York Giants in Super Bowl XXV.   **ABOVE**: James Lofton celebrates a touchdown during the 1991 playoffs.

Go-To Guys

To be a true star in the NFL, you need more than fast feet and a big body. You have to be a "go-to guy"—someone the coach wants on the field at the end of a big game. Bills fans have had a lot to cheer about over the years, including these great stars …

THE PIONEERS

BILLY SHAW   Offensive Lineman

• BORN: 12/15/1938   • PLAYED FOR TEAM: 1961 TO 1969

The Bills had a great running game in the 1960s, and Billy Shaw was the reason why. He was fast enough to lead rushing plays to the outside and big enough to block two or three men on one play. Shaw played in the **AFL All-Star Game** eight times in his nine seasons.

RON McDOLE   Defensive Lineman

• BORN: 9/9/1939   • PLAYED FOR TEAM: 1963 TO 1970

Ron McDole was the heart of the AFL's best defensive line with the Bills. He teamed with Tom Sestak, Jim Dunaway, and Tom Day to make it almost impossible for opponents to run the football. McDole **intercepted** 12 passes during his career—the most ever for a lineman.

COOKIE GILCHRIST Running Back

- BORN: 9/20/1935 • DIED: 1/10/2011
- PLAYED FOR TEAM: 1962 TO 1964

Cookie Gilchrist looked more like a linebacker than a running back. In his first season with the Bills, he became the first AFL player to rush for 1,000 yards.

JACK KEMP Quarterback

- BORN: 7/13/1935 • DIED: 5/2/2009
- PLAYED FOR TEAM: 1962 TO 1967 & 1969

Jack Kemp was a great leader and one of football's most athletic players. He led the Bills to the championship game three years in a row and was the AFL **Most Valuable Player (MVP)** in 1965. After retiring, he became a politician and ran for vice president of the United States in 1996.

O.J. SIMPSON Running Back

- BORN: 7/9/1947 • PLAYED FOR TEAM: 1969 TO 1977

O.J. Simpson was a fast and graceful runner who was impossible to tackle in the open field. When the Bills rehired Lou Saban to coach the team in 1972, he built his offense around Simpson. Over the next five years, the Juice led the NFL in rushing four times.

ABOVE: Cookie Gilchrist

ANDRE REED   Receiver

- BORN: 1/29/1964   • PLAYED FOR TEAM: 1985 TO 1999

Andre Reed was known for holding onto the ball after hard tackles and turning short passes into long plays. The speedy receiver led the AFC with 88 receptions in 1989. Reed caught 941 passes during his career for Buffalo.

BRUCE SMITH   Defensive Lineman

- BORN: 6/18/1963   • PLAYED FOR TEAM: 1985 TO 1999

Bruce Smith was the first choice in the 1985 NFL **draft**. The Bills never made a better pick. Smith was the heart of Buffalo's defense. Though he was usually double-teamed or triple-teamed, Smith recorded 171 sacks with the Bills.

JIM KELLY   Quarterback

- BORN: 2/14/1960   • PLAYED FOR TEAM: 1986 TO 1996

Jim Kelly's teammates used to joke that he played quarterback like a linebacker. His toughness and talent helped the Bills reach the playoffs eight times in 10 seasons. Kelly was a master of Buffalo's "K-gun no-huddle" offense, barking out plays right at the **line of scrimmage**.

CORNELIUS BENNETT   Linebacker

- BORN: 8/5/1965   • PLAYED FOR TEAM: 1987 TO 1995

When the Bills traded for Cornelius Bennett, they became a Super Bowl team. Bennett played behind Bruce Smith, and the pair terrorized opponents. Bennett was as effective stopping the run as he was sacking the quarterback.

THURMAN THOMAS   Running Back

- BORN: 5/16/1966
- PLAYED FOR TEAM: 1988 TO 1999

During his years with the Bills, Thurman Thomas was often the best player on the field. He gained 1,000 yards eight years in a row and caught 50 or more passes in four different seasons. Thomas was the AFC's top rusher three times.

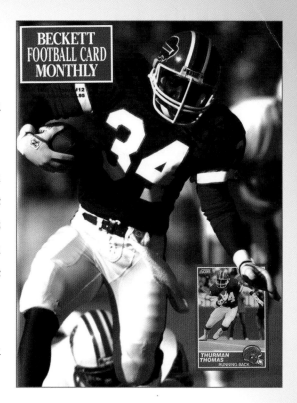

FRED JACKSON   Running Back

- BORN: 2/20/1981
- FIRST YEAR WITH TEAM: 2006

Fred Jackson came out of tiny Coe College. After several years on the bench for Buffalo, he developed into a star. In 2011, Jackson averaged more than six yards every time he touched the ball and scored on an 80-yard touchdown run.

STEVIE JOHNSON   Receiver

- BORN: 7/22/1986   • FIRST YEAR WITH TEAM: 2008

More than 200 players were drafted before the Bills picked Stevie Johnson in 2008. In 2010 and again in 2011, he caught more than 75 passes and gained over 1,000 yards. Johnson's touchdown celebrations reminded Buffalo fans that football can be as much fun to play as it is to watch.

ABOVE: Sports card collectors loved to read about Thurman Thomas.

Calling the Shots

When the Bills hire a head coach, they have high expectations. That's because Buffalo has had some of the best coaches in history. From 1962 to 1965—and again from 1972 to 1976—Lou Saban led the Bills. Saban matched quick blockers with big running backs such as Cookie Gilchrist and O.J. Simpson. Under Saban, the Bills had just two losing seasons, and they won the AFL championship twice.

When Buffalo began to struggle in the late 1970s, Chuck Knox took over the team and turned it around after just two seasons. He guided the Bills to the postseason twice. Like Saban, Knox believed in a powerful running game. The stars of Knox's teams were quarterback Joe Ferguson and running back Joe Cribbs. They gave Buffalo one of the most explosive offenses in the league.

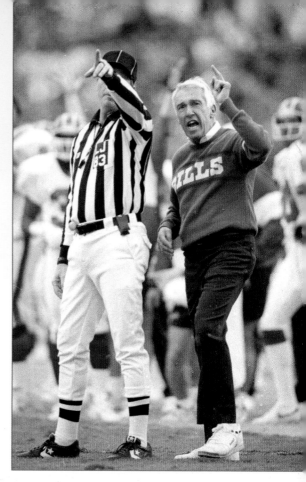

LEFT: Lou Saban celebrates a victory with his players.
RIGHT: Marv Levy has a difference of opinion with a referee.

The team's best coach was Marv Levy. When he took over the Bills in 1986, they had won only four games in two years. Levy was a believer in strong **special teams**. In many Buffalo victories, the kicker, punter, and other part-time players were the difference. That always made Levy very proud.

On offense and defense, Levy looked for quick, powerful players. Under his guidance, the Bills were always a very athletic team. They sent exciting stars to the **Pro Bowl** every year.

Levy guided the Bills to the Super Bowl four times. He designed a special offense that let quarterback Jim Kelly call plays right at the line of scrimmage. Often, the Bills skipped the huddle. This put great pressure on the defense to get set quickly. When opponents made a mistake, Kelly and teammates Thurman Thomas and Andre Reed usually took advantage of it.

One Great Day

When the 1973 season started, Buffalo fans expected great things from the Bills. Their star running back, O.J. Simpson, did not disappoint them. In the first game of the

year, he ran for 250 yards against the New England Patriots. By the season's seventh game, Simpson had reached 1,000 yards.

The record for most yards in a season at the time was 1,863. The great Jim Brown had set the mark 10 years earlier. Could O.J. beat it? With two games to go, Simpson had 1,584 yards. The Bills played the Patriots again, and he gained 219 yards. Now he was just 60 short of the record.

Buffalo's final game was against the New York Jets. The Jets knew they could not keep Simpson from breaking the old record, but

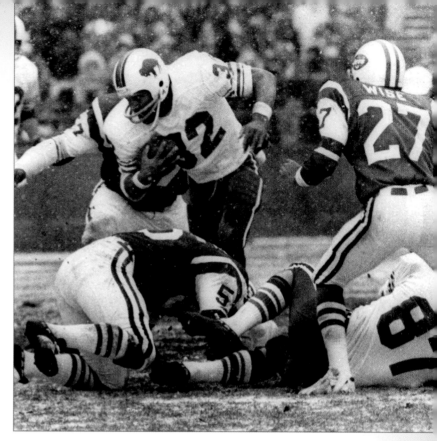

LEFT: O.J. Simpson signed this 1970s Sportscaster information card.
RIGHT: Simpson sets a new rushing record against the New York Jets.

they vowed they would not let him reach 2,000 yards. At game time, it looked as if the weather would help them. It was a drizzly day, and the field was muddy and slick.

Simpson surprised the Jets and got off to a great start. In fact, he smashed Brown's record before the second quarter began. No matter what New York tried, Simpson found holes in the defense.

Late in the fourth quarter, he took a handoff from Joe Ferguson and followed blockers Reggie McKenzie and Mike Montler as they blasted a hole through the left side on the line. By the time the Jets brought Simpson down, he had gained seven yards. It gave him 200 for the game and 2,003 for the season. After a pressure-packed season and a hard-fought game, Simpson was asked how he felt being the NFL's first 2,000-yard man. "Relieved," he said with a smile.

Legend Has It

Who had the best half-season in team history?

LEGEND HAS IT that Cornelius Bennett did. The Bills traded for the young linebacker in 1987 on Halloween. Bennett began his career as a substitute, but that didn't last long. He came off the bench in his first game and sacked the quarterback. After that, he was in the starting lineup. In eight games as a **rookie**, Bennett averaged a sack a game, and Buffalo became one of the best defensive teams in the AFC.

ABOVE: Cornelius Bennett takes on a big blocker.

Was Jack Kemp the best bargain in team history?

LEGEND HAS IT that he was. In 1962, the Bills paid $100 for Kemp after the San Diego Chargers placed him on **waivers**. The quarterback had injured his finger, and San Diego needed his spot on the roster for another player. What a mistake. The Bills claimed Kemp, and he led them to the AFL championship twice—both times over the Chargers!

Did Ryan Fitzpatrick have the best second half of a game in NFL history?

LEGEND HAS IT that he did. In their first home game of the 2011 season, the Bills hosted the Oakland Raiders. The fans could hardly believe it when Buffalo fell behind 21–3 after two quarters. But everything changed after halftime. Fitzpatrick led the Bills to an amazing 38–35 victory. He threw the winning touchdown pass with 14 seconds left on the clock. It was the first time in NFL history that a team scored offensive touchdowns five times in a row in the second half.

It Really Happened

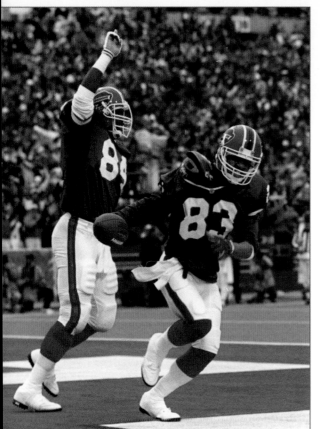

T he Bills' stadium can get very loud when Buffalo is winning. On January 3, 1993, it was deathly quiet. The 75,000 fans huddled in the stands that day for the team's playoff game against the Houston Oilers were ready to surrender.

The second half had barely begun, and the Bills were way behind, 35–3. To make matters worse, three of their best players—Jim Kelly, Thurman Thomas, and Cornelius Bennett— were injured and on the bench. It looked like Buffalo's season was over.

Frank Reich, in at quarterback for Kelly, did not agree. He led the Bills on a touchdown drive to make the score 35–10. Next, the Bills surprised Houston and recovered an **onside kick**. Reich then threw a long touchdown pass to Don Beebe. When Buffalo

LEFT: Andre Reed scores a touchdown against the Houston Oilers.
RIGHT: Frank Reich and Steve Christie jump for joy after the winning field goal.

got the ball back, Reich zipped a touchdown pass to Andre Reed. Suddenly, the crowd came alive.

After the Bills intercepted a pass, Reich and Reed connected in the end zone to make the score 35–31. Early in the fourth quarter, Reich hit Reed with another touchdown pass, and the Bills took the lead 38–35. When Houston tied the score with a last-second field goal, the game went into **overtime**.

The Buffalo crowd was louder than it had ever been as the extra period began. The Oilers were completely flustered at that point. The stadium practically exploded when the Bills intercepted another pass. Moments later, Steve Christie kicked a 32-yard field goal for a 41–38 victory and the greatest comeback in the history of the NFL playoffs.

Team Spirit

Buffalo fans root hard for the Bills regardless of the team's record. The Bills showed their appreciation for their fans in 1992 when they included the "12th Man" on their Wall of Fame. The 12th Man refers to the crowd, which can give the 11 players on the field an extra boost of energy by cheering as loud as possible.

Fans of the Bills are also known for their tailgating parties before games. Many people have been hosting fun events for more than 20 years. The food they serve is mouth-watering, especially the Buffalo wings. Bills fans have been eating these hot and spicy chicken treats for more than four *decades*.

Not everyone in the crowd at a Bills game is from Buffalo. Many fans come from across the border, in Canada. Some even make the trip from Toronto, which is three hours away on the opposite side of Lake Ontario.

LEFT: Nick Barnett gets a little love from the crowd in Buffalo.
ABOVE: Bills' fans wore this pin in the early 1960s.

Timeline

In this timeline, each Super Bowl is listed under the year it was played. Remember that the Super Bowl is held early in the year and is actually part of the previous season. For example, Super Bowl XLVI was played on February 5, 2012, but it was the championship of the 2011 NFL season.

1960
The Bills finish 5–8–1 in their first season.

1973
O.J. Simpson runs for 2,003 yards.

1964
The Bills win the AFL championship.

1977
Joe Ferguson leads the AFC in passing yards and completions.

1987
Shane Conlan is named NFL Defensive Rookie of the Year.

Tom Sestak starred for the Bills in their early years.

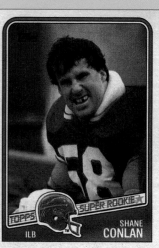

Shane Conlan

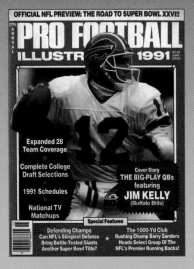

Jim
Kelly

Lee
Evans

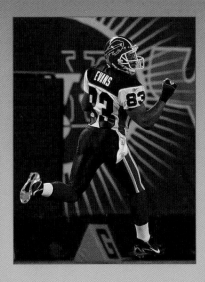

1994

The Bills reach the
Super Bowl for the
fourth year in a row.

1991

Jim Kelly leads the Bills
to their first Super Bowl.

2006

Lee Evans scores two 80-yard
touchdowns in the same quarter.

1988

Fred Smerlas plays
in his fifth Pro Bowl.

2011

The Bills score five second-half
touchdowns to beat the Oakland Raiders.

Fred Smerlas was the
heart of the Buffalo
defense in the 1980s.

Fun Facts

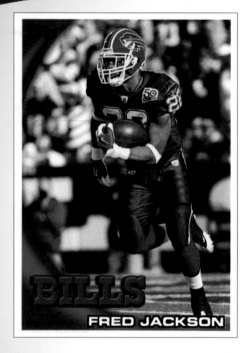

FRED JACKSON

ACTION JACKSON

When Fred Jackson was in high school, he was never a starter. How things change! In 2009, he became the first NFL player to have 1,000 rushing yards and 1,000 kickoff return yards in the same season.

A LEG UP

When the Bills drafted Pete Gogolak in 1964, he became the first **soccer-style** kicker in pro football. In his first game for Buffalo, in the preseason against the New York Jets, he booted a 57-yard field goal. The NFL record at the time was 56 yards.

TURNING THE TABLES

In a 2010 game against the Cincinnati Bengals, the Bills trailed 31–14 at halftime. They ended up winning 49–31. It was the first time a team had ever been behind by 17 points and won by 18 or more.

DEEP THREAT

In 1964, receiver Elbert Dubenion averaged 27.1 yards per catch. No one with 40 or more catches has ever done better. Dubenion's nickname was "Golden Wheels."

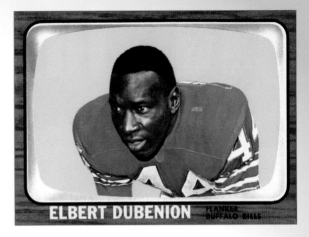

ELBERT DUBENION   FLANKER BUFFALO BILLS

DO NOT ENTER

During the 1960s, the Bills took great pride in their ability to stop the running game. From 1964 to 1965, Buffalo went 17 games in a row without allowing a rushing touchdown.

21ST CENTURY MEN

The Bills have had great luck finding good running backs. From 2002 to 2009, four different runners gained more than 1,000 yards in one season for the team—Travis Henry, Willis McGahee, Marshawn Lynch, and Fred Jackson.

FAMOUS FIRST

In 1969, James Harris opened the year as Buffalo's quarterback. It marked the first time an African American began a season as his team's starter at that position.

LEFT: Fred Jackson   **ABOVE**: Elbert Dubenion

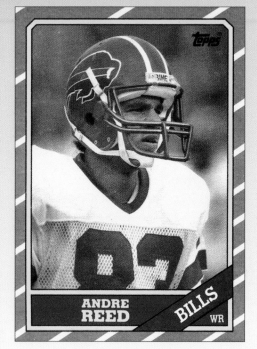

ANDRE
REED · BILLS
WR

"We believed in each other. We had each others' backs."
► **Andre Reed,** *on how the Bills made it to the Super Bowl four years in a row*

"He never missed a practice, never missed a game, never did anything to hurt the team on or off the field. He was really the **conscience** of the team."
► **Steve Tasker,** *on the role Thurman Thomas played in the Buffalo locker room*

"Their hearts were as warm as the thermal underwear I wore during the playoff games!"
► **Marv Levy,** *on the fans who came out to watch the Bills in cold weather*

"No man is more important than the team."
► **Stevie Johnson,** *on what a star player must always remember*

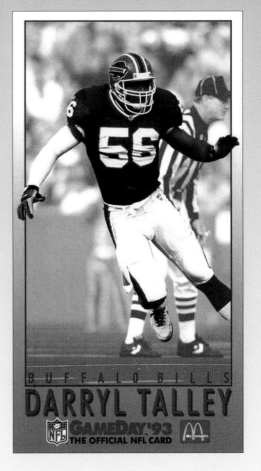

"I knew the guy had a tremendous amount of talent and I wasn't going to sit there and let it go to waste."

▶ *Darryl Talley,* *on why he pushed Bruce Smith so hard as a rookie*

"Whenever we need a play, he seems to be making the play, whether it's in the pass game or running the ball or breaking five tackles. I can't say enough about him."

▶ *Ryan Fitzpatrick,* *on Fred Jackson*

"You never saw fear in his eyes. You always saw confidence. That's what made Jack the man he was: his ability to rise to the occasion."

▶ *Billy Shaw,* *on Jack Kemp*

"For a guy his size, there was no one stronger. Pound-for-pound, he was the strongest guy I've ever seen."

▶ *Joe DeLamielleure,* *on Joe Ferguson*

LEFT: Andre Reed
ABOVE: Darryl Talley

Great Debates

People who root for the Bills love to compare their favorite moments, teams, and players. Some debates have been going on for years! How would you settle these classic football arguments?

The Bills of the 1960s would beat the Bills of the 1990s ...

... because they were the champions of the AFL—twice in a row! Jack Kemp completed passes all over the field. Cookie Gilchrist plowed through tacklers for big gains. The defense slammed the door on almost every opponent. The Bills of the 1960s were an excellent *all-around* team that won in many different ways.

No way! The Bills of the 1990s would have destroyed those old Buffalo clubs ...

... because they had more talent at every single position. Jim Kelly was better than Kemp, Thurman Thomas (   ) was better than Gilchrist, and no one could have covered Andre Reed. Both teams had great defenses, but no one scared opposing offenses more than Bruce Smith. A game between these two squads might be close, but coach Marv Levy would find a way to win every time.

O.J. Simpson was the best running back in team history ...

... because he was the first and only player to gain 2,000 yards in a 14-game season. The Juice had good size, tremendous speed, and incredible moves. When Simpson (RIGHT) joined the Bills in 1969, fans were amazed when a running back finished a season with 1,000 yards. In 1973, Simpson had 2,003 yards!

Sorry. Thurman Thomas was a much more valuable player ...

... because he did everything a great running back was supposed to do—and more. Between his carries and catches, Thomas led the NFL in total yards from scrimmage four

FOOTBALL REGISTER

O. J. SIMPSON
Buffalo Bills

PUBLISHED BY
The Sporting News
1974

times. No one else has ever done that. He was also the best player on the field in Super Bowl XXV, but a missed field goal at the end of the game kept him from being named the game's MVP. Most important of all, Thomas was a team leader. He led both by words and by example.

For the Record

T he great Bills teams and players have left their marks on the record books. These are the "best of the best" …

Bruce Smith

Jim Kelly

BILLS AWARD WINNERS

WINNER	AWARD	YEAR
Cookie Gilchrist	AFL co-MVP	1962
Jack Kemp	AFL co-MVP	1962
Lou Saban	AFL Coach of the Year	1964
Lou Saban	AFL Coach of the Year	1965
O.J. Simpson	Pro Bowl MVP	1973
O.J. Simpson	NFL Offensive Player of the Year	1973
O.J. Simpson	NFL Most Valuable Player	1973
Jim Haslett	NFL Defensive Rookie of the Year	1979
Chuck Knox	NFL Coach of the Year	1980
Shane Conlan	NFL Defensive Rookie of the Year	1987
Bruce Smith	Pro Bowl MVP	1988
Bruce Smith	NFL Defensive Player of the Year	1990
Thurman Thomas	NFL Offensive Player of the Year	1991
Thurman Thomas	NFL Most Valuable Player	1991
Jim Kelly	Pro Bowl MVP	1991
Steve Tasker	Pro Bowl MVP	1993
Bryce Paup	NFL Defensive Player of the Year	1995
Bruce Smith	NFL Defensive Player of the Year	1996
Doug Flutie	NFL Comeback Player of the Year	1998

BILLS ACHIEVEMENTS

ACHIEVEMENT	YEAR
AFL East Champions	1964
AFL Champions	1964
AFL East Champions	1965
AFL Champions	1965
AFL East Champions	1966
AFC East Champions	1980
AFC East Champions	1988
AFC East Champions	1989
AFC East Champions	1990
AFC Champions	1990
AFC East Champions	1991
AFC Champions	1991
AFC Champions	1992
AFC East Champions	1993
AFC Champions	1993
AFC East Champions	1995

BUFFALO

STEW BARBER tackle

ABOVE: Stew Barber was a star for Buffalo's great AFL teams of the 1960s.
LEFT: Reggie McKenzie anchored the offensive line for the 1980 Bills.

Pinpoints

The history of a football team is made up of many smaller stories. These stories take place all over the map—not just in the city a team calls "home." Match the pushpins on these maps to the **Team Facts**, and you will begin to see the story of the Bills unfold!

TEAM FACTS

1. Buffalo, New York—*The Bills have played here since 1960.*
2. Pittsburgh, Pennsylvania—*Jim Kelly was born here.*
3. Norfolk, Virginia—*Bruce Smith was born here.*
4. Detroit, Michigan—*Reggie McKenzie was born here.*
5. Chicago, Illinois—*Marv Levy was born here.*
6. Vonore, Tennessee—*Mike Stratton was born here.*
7. Canton, Ohio—*George Saimes was born here.*
8. Miami, Florida—*The Bills won the 1992 AFC championship here.*

Joe Ferguson

9. Alvin, Texas—*Joe Ferguson was born here.*
10. San Diego, California—*The Bills won the 1965 AFL championship here.*
11. San Francisco, California—*O.J. Simpson was born here.*
12. Budapest, Hungary—*Pete Gogolak was born here.*

Glossary

🧠 **Football Words**
👥 **Vocabulary Words**

AFL ALL-STAR GAME—The annual game that featured the AFL's best players.

AFL CHAMPIONSHIP GAME—The game that decided the winner of the AFL.

ALL-AMERICA FOOTBALL CONFERENCE (AAFC)—The professional league that played for four seasons, from 1946 to 1949.

ALL-AROUND—Good at many different parts of the game.

AMERICAN FOOTBALL CONFERENCE (AFC)—One of two groups of teams that make up the NFL. The winner of the AFC plays the winner of the National Football Conference (NFC) in the Super Bowl.

AMERICAN FOOTBALL LEAGUE (AFL)—The football league that began play in 1960 and later merged with the NFL.

CONSCIENCE—A feeling or judgment that helps someone tell right from wrong.

DECADES—Periods of 10 years; also specific periods, such as the 1950s.

DRAFT—The annual meeting during which NFL teams choose from a group of the best college players.

FIELD GOALS—Goals from the field, kicked over the crossbar and between the goal posts. A field goal is worth three points.

FINANCE—Contribute money.

INTERCEPTED—Caught in the air by a defensive player.

LINE OF SCRIMMAGE—The imaginary line that separates the offense and defense before each play begins.

MODERNIZED—Brought up to date.

MOST VALUABLE PLAYER (MVP)—The award given each year to the league's best player; also given to the best player in the Super Bowl and Pro Bowl.

NATIONAL FOOTBALL LEAGUE (NFL)—The league that started in 1920 and is still operating today.

ONSIDE KICK—A short kickoff that the kicking team tries to recover.

OVERTIME—The extra period played when a game is tied after 60 minutes.

PLAYOFFS—The games played after the regular season to determine which teams play in the Super Bowl.

POSTSEASON—Another term for playoffs.

PRO BOWL—The NFL's all-star game, played after the regular season.

PROFESSIONAL—Paid to play.

QUARTERBACK SNEAK—A play where the quarterback keeps the ball and tries to "sneak" past the defensive line.

ROOKIE—A player in his first year.

SACK—Tackle of the quarterback behind the line of scrimmage.

SECONDARY—The part of the defense made up by the cornerbacks and safeties.

SOCCER-STYLE—Approaching the ball on an angle instead of straight on.

SPECIAL TEAMS—The groups of players who take the field for punts, kickoffs, field goals, and extra points.

STRATEGY—A plan or method for succeeding.

SUPER BOWL—The championship of the NFL, played between the winners of the NFC and AFC.

WAIVERS—A list of players who have been released by their teams.

OVERTIME

TEAM SPIRIT introduces a great way to stay up to date with your team! Visit our **OVERTIME** link and get connected to the latest and greatest updates. **OVERTIME** serves as a young reader's ticket to an exclusive web page—with more stories, fun facts, team records, and photos of the Bills. Content is updated during and after each season. The **OVERTIME** feature also enables readers to send comments and letters to the author!

Log onto:

www.norwoodhousepress.com/library.aspx

and click on the tab: **TEAM SPIRIT** to access **OVERTIME**.

Read all the books in the series to learn more about professional sports. For a complete listing of the baseball, basketball, football, and hockey teams in the **TEAM SPIRIT** series, visit our website at:

www.norwoodhousepress.com/library.aspx

On the Road

BUFFALO BILLS
One Bills Drive
Orchard Park, New York 14127
716-648-1800
www.buffalobills.com

THE PRO FOOTBALL HALL OF FAME
2121 George Halas Drive NW
Canton, Ohio 44708
330-456-8207
www.profootballhof.com

On the Bookshelf

To learn more about the sport of football, look for these books at your library or bookstore:

- Frederick, Shane. *The Best of Everything Football Book.* North Mankato, Minnesota: Capstone Press, 2011.

- Jacobs, Greg. *The Everything Kids' Football Book: The All-Time Greats, Legendary Teams, Today's Superstars—And Tips on Playing Like a Pro.* Avon, Massachusetts: Adams Media Corporation, 2010.

- Editors of *Sports Illustrated for Kids. 1st and 10: Top 10 Lists of Everything in Football.* New York, New York: Sports Illustrated Books, 2011.

Index

PAGE NUMBERS IN **BOLD** REFER TO ILLUSTRATIONS.

About the Author

MARK STEWART has written more than 50 books on football and over 150 sports books for kids. He grew up in New York City during the 1960s rooting for the Giants and Jets, and was lucky enough to meet players from both teams. Mark comes from a family of writers. His grandfather was Sunday Editor of *The New York Times,* and his mother was Articles Editor of *Ladies' Home Journal* and *McCall's.* Mark has profiled hundreds of athletes over the past 25 years. He has also written several books about his native New York and New Jersey, his home today. Mark is a graduate of Duke University, with a degree in history. He lives and works in a home overlooking Sandy Hook, New Jersey. You can contact Mark through the Norwood House Press website.